T0131702

It's Funny You'll See From A #2 Z

David L. Mitchell

Rev. date: 10/03/2018

Print information available on the last page.

Orders@Xlibris.com
www.Xlibris.com
1-888-795-4274
Xlibris
To order additional copies of this book, contact:

ISBN: Softcover   978-1-4010-7905-5
         EBook   978-1-4691-2449-0

- I dedicate this book to my mother

"IT's Funny You'll SEE From A #2 Z

"HELLO" Boyz and Girlz LETs began To have loads OF FUN UNDER the SUN while LEARNING COOL NEW WORDs FROM A#2Z while looking AT COlorFul AND Comical Pictures THAT will make you Laugh AND THAT you'll SEE AND BEFore you Finish you'll BE Smarter AND HAPPY.

This IS A Unique "Hip Hop" Primer For All To ENjoy IT's SO GREAT you Could CAll iT A Toy HOWEVER IT's MorE THEN THAT IT's ALSO A LEARNING TööL For HOME OR Schööl

"IT'S FUNNY You"ll SEE From A #2 Z IS A SENSATIONAL LitERAry AND Art PiecE And IT would BE A PerFect GiFT For your Son, DAughter, NEphEW, OR NiECE.

"I ENCOURAGE EVERYONE who has A TASTE FOR LEARNING AND Who LOVES #2 LAugh #2 GET AND Support "IT'S Funny You'll SEE From A #2 Z BECAUSE you"ll HAVE ONE Big GREAT PARTY...

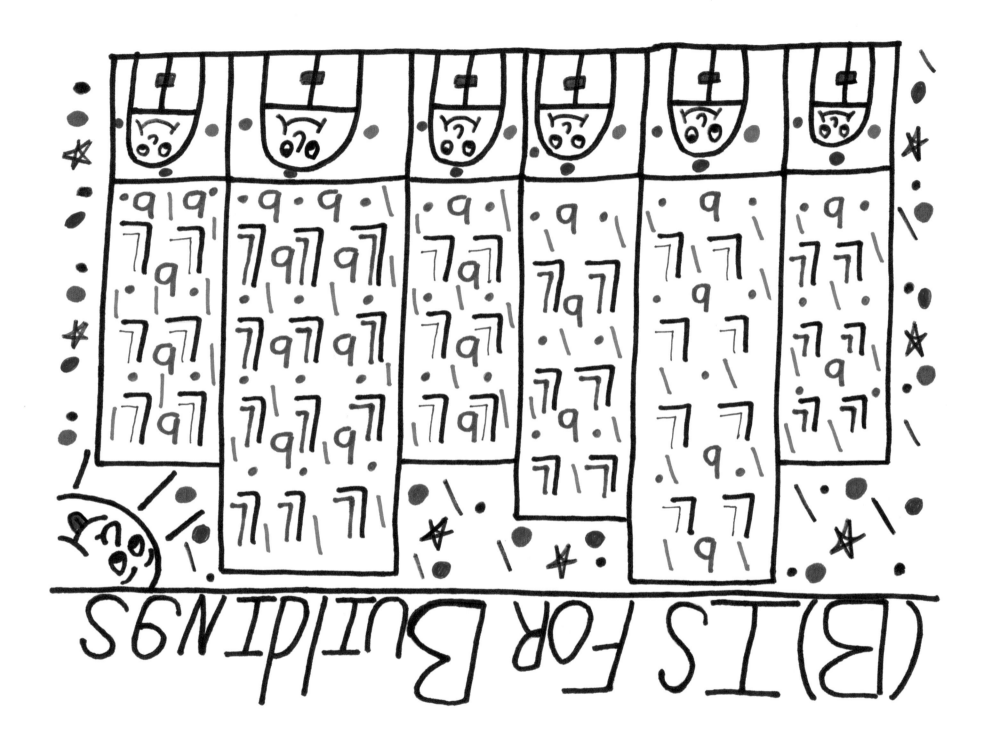

(B)IS FoR BuidiNgS

(C) IS FOR COMPUTER

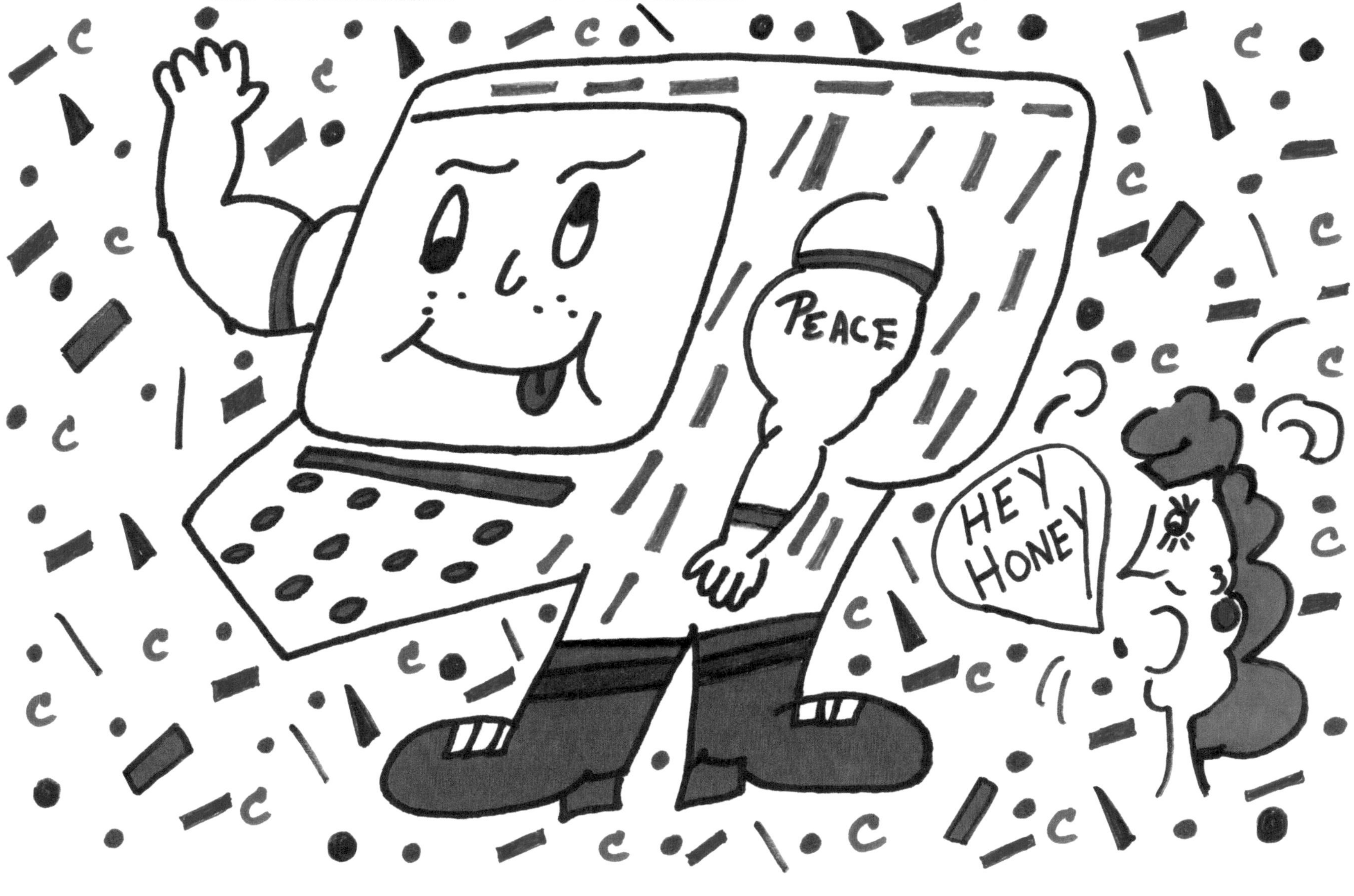

(D)IS FOR DIAMOND

(E) IS FOR EYE

(G) IS FOR GIFT

(H)IS FOR HEART

(J) IS FOR JERSEY

(K) IS FOR KEY

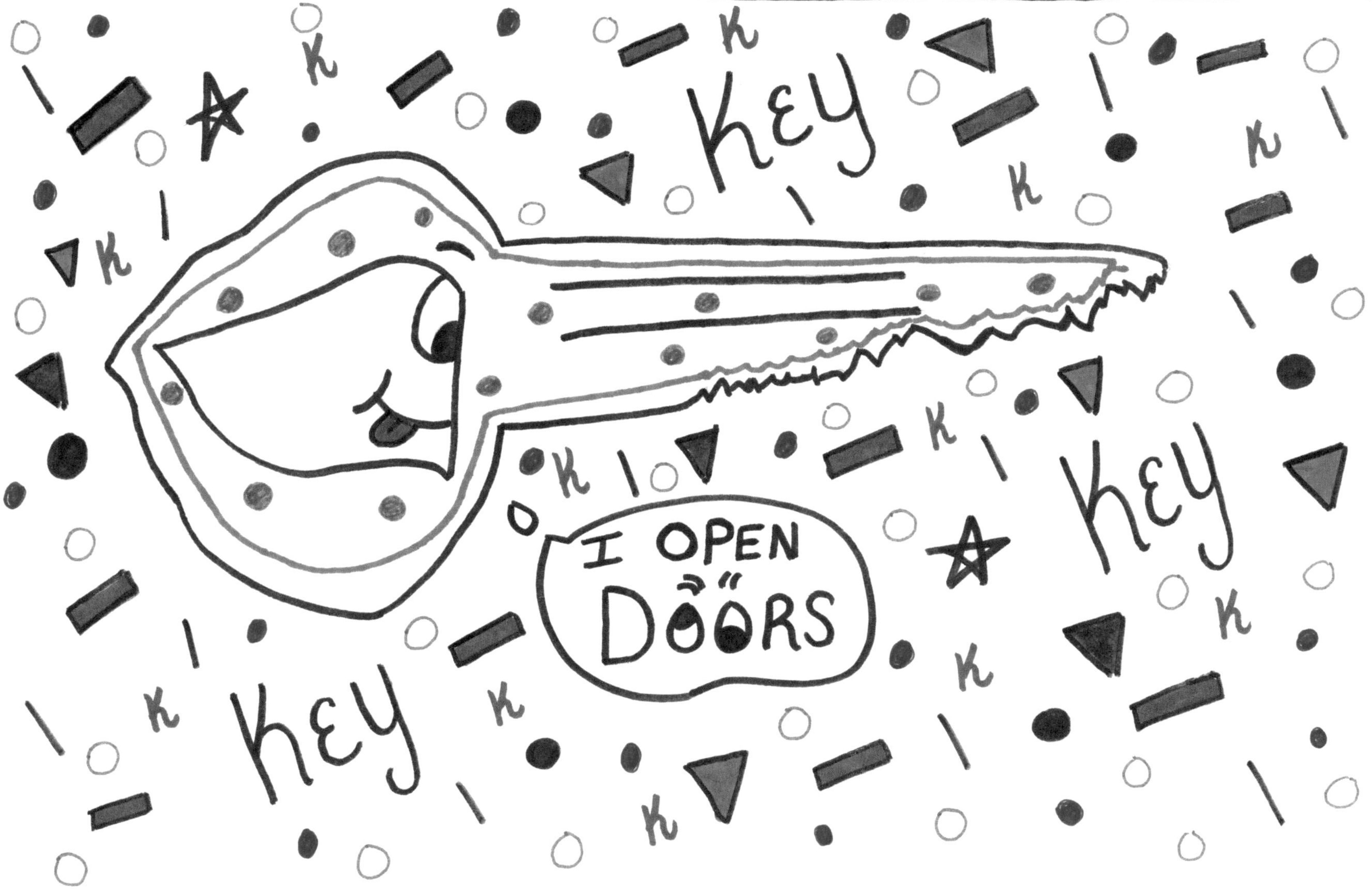

(L)IS FOR LÖCK

(M) IS FOR MONEY

(N) IS FOR NUMBERS

(P) IS FOR PIZZA

(R) IS FOR KING

(S) Is For STARS

(U) Is For Umbrella

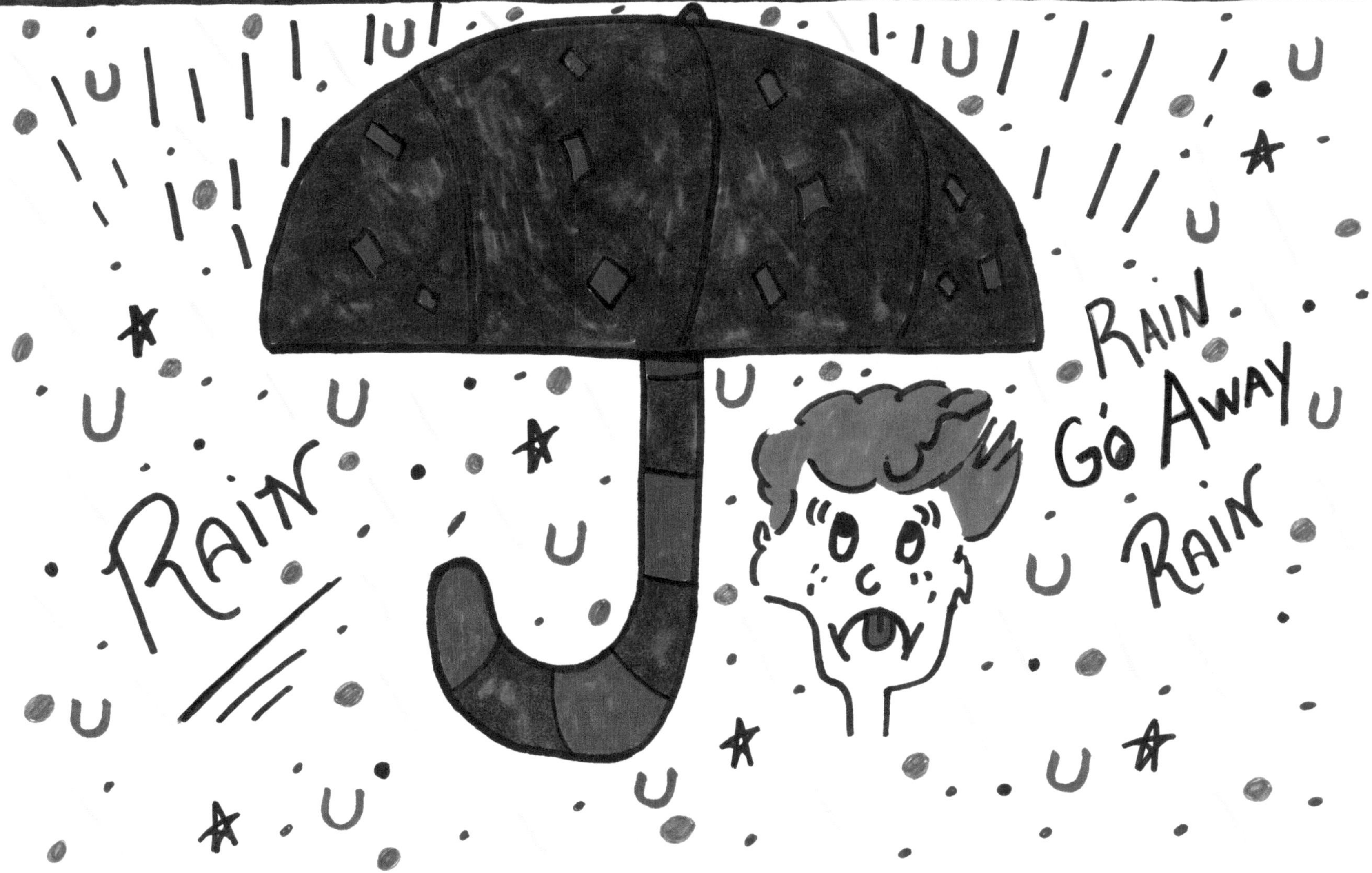

(W) IS FOR WATCH

THE TIME

THE TIME

THE TIME

IT IS 9:15 Kids

(X) IS FOR XRAY

ThaTS ME

HEY Dude

(Z) IS FOR ZERO

Printed in the United States
By Bookmasters